The Nymph
of the
Unknown Forest

The Nymph
of the
Unknown Forest

(Collection of Poems)

By
Loni Hoots

Middle Island Press
2015

Published by Middle Island Press
PO Box 354
West Union, WV 26456

Dedicated to my parents
Cindy and David.
Dedicated to my aunt Jennie.
She has always believed in me
and my writing. And dedicated
to everyone around the world
who has inspired my writings.

Contents

The Nymph
of the Unknown Forest

The Trees

Out here on this isolated road,

I'm completely lost.

The sky is covered with thick clouds,

Shielding the light away from me,

Making it harder to see.

I'm surrounded by the trees and falling leaves.

The smell of fall is in the air.

And the coolness of the wind is starting to settle in.

Out of the corner of my eye,

I see a village surrounding a couple of trees.

As I inch closer, I get smaller.

I approach an old man.

His eyes are dark blue and he has pointy ears.

"Welcome, my dear."

I'm taken to a small home

and rest for the night.

Tomorrow, I shall venture some more.

Black Eyes

As I stare into the murky waters below my feet,

I sense a pair of eyes staring at me.

For some unknown reason I don't understand

What came over me.

I looked up and saw two black eyes peering from the

murky waters.

Closing my eyes, I prayed that I was imagining.

Opened my eyes and the two black eyes were a few

inches away from me.

I glanced towards the river bank,

Staring at a black cherry tree.

Wishing that I could escape the stare of the black eyes.

But nothing would rescue me,

For I felt something licking upon my leg.

Frozen still, my skin went pale.

I could feel myself shaking.

Another lick upon my leg,

At this point I don't know what to think.

Out of nowhere, something wraps itself around my leg.

I'm pulled down by a great force.

Under the water I can't breathe,

And there is no hope to be free.

Suffocating and water pouring down my throat.

I awake to see a person staring at me.

I look at my reflection in the water.

I now have black eyes and I am part of the

                              murky waters.

The Mermaid of the Moon

I sit here on the edge of the cave,

Looking over the ocean.

The clouds are slowly creeping over the moon.

No stars are out tonight.

A light breeze gently kisses my skin,

And the smell of the ocean water fills my lungs.

I feel safe and at home.

I hear a small splash below my feet.

Looking down, I see a orange-silver tail going back

                          into the water.

Then a face appears.

Her hair is jet black,

Eyes are blue,

And skin is pale.

The sweet young lady smiled and waved.

She dove back into the depths of the ocean.

The orange-silver tail followed her.

Then I realized

She was the legendary mermaid of the moon.

Now, this mermaid haunts my dreams.

The Water Spirit

As I sit here in the bath,

The soapy water flows over my body.

I lift my legs above the water,

But my legs are not there.

In my legs place,

There is a white tail with purple specks all over.

The tail is smooth and slimy.

It starts at my hips and ends where my feet should be.

The water flows over my bosom.

It wades back and forth,

As if it is using the ocean current.

A purple and white necklace suddenly appears,

Flowing over my bosom.

I stay in the bath just for a few more minutes.

I don't want this to end.

I sit up and unplug the bath.

The water goes down the drain.

For just a moment the tail is still there.

Then the tail vanishes,

As well as the necklace.

I can't wait to be in the water again.

For I am the water spirit.

Bali's Water Spirit

The rain falls down heavily,

Turning the dirt road into a muddy one.

The mountain backdrop is covered in a rainy mist.

I stand in the doorway

With my purple dress on,

And slippers on my feet.

I put a protection spell on me,

So the water doesn't turn me.

But that doesn't work.

The moment I step out onto the muddy road,

A mist forms over my feet.

Suddenly the mist gently covers my body.

I walk down the road,

And no one notices the mist around my body.

I walk towards the forest

While the rain pours down.

The leaves look beautiful with rain falling on them.

I walk deeper into the rainy forest,

And start to slowly vanish into the rain.

Guardians of the Garden

As I stand here out in the courtyard,

Looking at the star filled night sky.

My gown clings to my body,

As the gentle wind pushes against me.

Owls hooting.

Crickets chirping.

I can hear the slight ripple of the waterfall going into

the lake nearby.

Out of the corner of my eye,

I see a dozen glowing lights.

All of the lights in the garden dance around the

flowers and herbs.

I hear little giggles coming from the garden.

I inch closer to the garden,

The lights get lighter.

And bodies form.

Sweet faces of boys and girls.

Tiny bodies.

They greet me with a smile and an anise.

A warrior fighting around the roses.

Daughter of the Moon

Her hair is black like the night sky.

Her eyes are deep blue like the bottom of the sea.

The light purple satin dress flows freely around her body.

I stand a few feet away,

Watching her move slowly towards the moonlight.

I hear a whisper, "count back from ten."

So I began.

10, 9, 8, 7, 6, 5, 4, 3, 2, 1.

Right before my eyes she was gone.

The moon took her.

But I noticed she left a token.

A little piece of paper left for me.

A note telling me "to be me."

Munduk

As I stand here on the ridges of Munduk,

I can smell the rain beginning to fall.

It hasn't touched my skin,

But the smell of the rain is undeniable.

The birds chirp

As they fly above my head.

The sounds of other animals fill the fog as it lingers

in the morning sky.

Away from bustling cities.

Away from corrupt civilization.

This is my home.

My home away from the rest of the world.

Munduk is my place.

Munduk is my home.

Welcome to the hidden hills.

Welcome to the place that's unknown.

Gentle Waves

Her gentle waves wash over my feet.

Her soft whispers brush my skin.

Here I stand on the edge of the beach,

Watching all the birds fly away while singing in harmony.

Her gentle waves roll in.

So quiet, so peaceful.

Far off in the distance.

Past the rocks.

The fish come up and talk.

Oh her gentle waves capture my heart.

Her waves put me in a trance.

Unbreakable trance.

Fountain

This sweet place,

Of green and peace.

Not a sound can be heard,

Not from a mile or more.

Oh sweet serenity fill me up, fill me up with your

majestic sounds.

Not far up ahead a beautiful fountain lies.

On this bright and sunny Day,

The water glistens with sunlight.

Inching closer, I can see flowers are blooming.

Roses, lilacs, and tulips.

Oh can there be anything more beautiful?

I feel as though I am on the edge of the cliff.

Looking down,

And taking it all in.

This fountain,

You give me such dreams.

Such sweet, precious dreams.

Palace in the Ocean

My heart pitter-patters on the floor,

But my mind is already out the door.

My body sways back and forth

As the ocean waves wash me back to shore.

Lost for several days in the ocean.

Quiet, peaceful, as I listen to the waves

While I drift away.

I'm sucked back into the water.

Onto the ocean floor.

I see beautiful starfish scattered all around.

A beautiful statue just a few miles ahead.

So I began to swim.

A school of fish swims right by.

They look majestic in my eye.

This magnificent place I see before me.

This palace that sits right next to me.

The steps are broken but not lost.

I would stay here forever,

Even if I were forced back.

Stuck in the past.

Watching the misty dancers begin to dance.

I drift away once more,

But this time towards the door and not the shore.

Raindrops in the Ocean

If only for a day I could stay here.

Where I can just put my feet up,

And watch the waves rock back and forth.

Where no problems can come my way.

Stuck in a boat,

Floating out into the sea.

I am far away.

This is where I can right my wrongs.

As the wind picks up,

I still see no land.

And that's alright by me.

Raindrops begin to fall,

I lay back down on the boat looking up into the sky.

All of my problems are starting to fade away.

The breeze still is cool.

But no worries.

Raindrops fall back into the ocean.

My dress is soaked.

Nothing is wrong with me.

This is the way I let my problems fade away.

The boat gently touches the land and I suddenly realize

That all of my problems are gone.

Raindrops fall back against the misty backdrop,

Falling into the gentle waves.

Night Sky

The wind takes charge,

Blowing in a frenzy.

Rocks the top of the trees.

As I sit on the patio,

My hair flows back.

The wind rushes throughout the night sky.

Cloudy sky.

No stars or moon out tonight.

The sleepy little town just doesn't care.

Everything is laid out and bare.

My weight supports my body.

Yet as if the wind has a powerful force, tries and tries

to pick me up.

Oh how I love the breeze,

It brings shivers down my spine.

A delightful taste for my mind.

I seclude myself in one spot.

Away from the world.

Listen to the birds and to the nighttime life.

Everyone safe,

Tucked in their beds,

While I stay out here till the night ends.

Lost to the Sea

The roaring of the waves comes to the beach.

It draws me in.

The calm water whispers, "take a dip."

I smile.

Oh visions of waters sweep through my mind.

I'm lost.

Visions of dancing beneath the water grave have

                              taken over my eyes,

I keep trying to mimic them.

So graceful.

So pure.

Such lovely pictures.

I'm lost to the sea.

But my heart is still free.

For she has no words of how in awe she is.

Take one more breath,

And down with the ship I go.

Shadows

The night carelessly picks me up.

Violently shaking me.

Rattling all of my bones.

The feelings of my heart begin to break.

I know that tonight will be an adventure.

The thunder shakes throughout the sky.

My heart skips a beat.

Shadows lurk,

Trying to descend onto me.

The blackness covers the four walls that surround

my soul.

Trapping me inside.

Captivated.

Prisoner in my own guilt.

Slave to the darkness.

Chained to the wall like some rabid animal,

Never to escape.

Yet somehow it seems to calm me down.

The shadows sweep over me and silently trap me

in its arms.

Balcony of Love

As I sit here on this balcony,

I look up at the star-filled night sky.

A soft whisper fills the wind, "My dear, look down."

As I stand up, I see a pair of eyes looking at me.

He is a gorgeous man.

Curly raven hair.

Bright green eyes.

Soft lips.

My hand reaches for his.

I bring him over the balcony.

As we stand there,

We stare into each other's eyes,

Capturing the moment.

His hands caress my waist,

Inching me closer to him.

Leaning forward, I gently kiss hiss lips.

Oh, I knew 'tis true.

So soft.

Losing myself,

I give into him.

As he does to me.

I pull away and whisper, "Good night."

"Good night, my love."

I close my eyes,

Then open them again.

He's gone for the night.

Lady Morgana

Her long black curly hair frames her face.

Her bright blue eyes shine brightly against her pale face.

Her stare can switch from warm to dead within seconds.

To cross her path could end in deadly consequence.

Her mind is sharp.

Her heart is powerful.

Just the same way her powers run through her hands.

Once a friend,

Now enemy.

One must keep an eye on her closely.

Although she is everyone's enemy.

She will be evermore my friend,

No matter how powerful she may be.

Lady Morgana will be the most powerful queen,

Powerful queen in ancient history.

Keeping the Meadows Alive

The beautiful meadows are filled with red roses.

The softness of the grass under her feet tickled her

                                                    lightly.

Softly taking steps,

She didn't want to ruin the landscape.

She wanted to preserve the flowers.

Let them fully bloom.

Once they had fully bloomed,

She would then pick them.

Carry them off to her villa.

For now, these roses will stay.

Stay to keep the meadows alive.

Biography

Loni Hoots has always been a writer, more specifically a poet. As she was growing up, she would always be writing poems and short stories in her classes instead of paying attention. At the age of 23, Loni has already written well over two hundred poems. Some of them are shared on her blog, and others locked away for right now. Inspiration comes from everywhere and everyone. It is hard to tear a journal and pen away from her.

Loni spent her early life in Colorado and now travels all over America. She has a blog site: The Healing Garden.